THORN HOUSE

THOM SCHRAMM

Yas Press
University of New Hampshire
English Department
230 Hamilton Smith Hall
Durham, NH 03824
Managing Editor: Danielle Jones

Published in partnership with Pink Eraser Press
Cover and interior designer: Ashley Halsey
Managing editor: Molly McGrath

Printed in the USA

CONTENTS

)(

INTRODUCTION

When judging a book contest, every judge hopes for a book that grabs their attention and refuses to let go. *Thorn House* by Thom Schramm, with its abundance of skillfully wrought music and its wrecked, unruly heart, stood out to me in this way. This is a collection that enthralls the reader from the lyrical hypnosis of the very first poem, weaving a spell that propels us through the book's entirety. As the title suggests, we are both damaged and sheltered by these poems, scratched and bloodied by their barbed circumstances even as we are comforted by their softness. The poems place us inside a New Hampshire wood both sinister and beautiful until *Thorn House* becomes a book of fairy tales that guide us through to an oven, to a stranger's bed, to a long deep sleep.

In *Thorn House*, the domestic is treacherous and the dangerous is home. An unspoken understanding between reader and speaker exists—we are in the church of the wound or the scratch or the scrape—as clipped, careful moments tug against the chaos at the edge of each poem. Schramm's opening poem shows a speaker seeking to "hatch" and to "heal" from the past. By the book's final piece, the cumulative damage is a literal crack down the center of a poem that finally heals by its end. This is a book thick with New England graveyards, bloodied birch trees, forest pathways lined with the hung bodies of trapped rabbits. At the heart of each line and stanza sits the New Hampshire wilderness, a place of cold and remoteness and wonder, a place that offers refuge from family but also its own dangers. In "Wake: 1978," the arrival of an ice cream truck is juxtaposed with a dead child lying in a living room coffin. In "In Silence," snakes emerge from a concrete set of steps poured badly. And in "Yesterday I Wrote a Poem Called 'Yesterday,'" Mother preaches "her strictures, scriptures that were best obeyed." In several poems, including "Hide and Seek," children disappear into the woods and are unable to be found. The parents in the collection are shadowy figures who are sometimes avoided or escaped.

Poems of family and damage in *Thorn House* are balanced by a quieter series of eight 19-line poems centered around a correspondence with former New Hampshire Poet Laureate Jane Kenyon both before and during her illness. These poems capture moments of intimacy and fear and add to the foreboding sense of the collection, the feeling that we are in a darkness of the woods edged by the comfort of connection. As we read snippets of letters, caring inquiries and sentiments, and the news of her illness and decline, we see how the pain of two people can bond them together. Kenyon's cursive is "small, like nerve endings." Her pain is a *"bone pain"* suffered for too long. A reaching out across miles and silences becomes clear, as does the urgency of connection. Then finally the news of Kenyon's leukemia breaks, and a postscript to the exchange depicts a reflection at Kenyon's grave in Andover, New Hampshire, in a silence of snow.

Thorn House moves toward its conclusion with additional compelling poems whose subjects pull us along. As we near the book's conclusion, Schramm writes a sound rejection of the Lamborghini, citing, "I refuse to look at Lamborghinis, / because Lamborghinis are driven / to be seen." He fleshes out a suicide hotline protocol in an instructional poem, while acknowledging that "you can never understand / their loss by following the protocols / you know." There are poems featuring the physics of skiing moguls and maidenhair ferns as "ragged shocks of hair" that "creep / like zombies."

In the end, *Thorn House* is a book built upon the dichotomy promised in its title. The northern wildernesses of our days offer both refuge and threat. We are housed in these poems that skim a discomfort just below the surface. There is something in us that rocks in the cradle of this book's music and is soothed. We know that every house is in some ways a house made of thorns, and yet now, with this excellent writing, this incredible ordering of the chaos through music and line break and image and carefully rendered line, we are finally out of the woods.

Jennifer Militello
New Hampshire Poet Laureate
Judge of the 2025 Granite State Poetry Prize

Yesterday I Wrote A Poem Called "Yesterday"

The lines I used were basically the same.
The one that read, *My blue eggs never hatched,*
was fabricated, yarn of passion, play.
I never laid an egg. I never lived
a past, unmitigated life. (I think.)

Of course, there was that time my childhood stopped
its beating—Mother sat me down to preach
her strictures, scriptures that were best obeyed.
The empty house resounded with my guilt—

until the tongues that rang that bell were stilled
by friction. Echoes carried, though "unreal."
So many years have passed it's hard to know
what happened. Sad. If only lives were taped...

Perhaps the past's a gift best left untapped,
an abstract bath of facts for us to form
from. Context matters, facts will shift, but still
at times I appeal to peals of the past
to heal, to hatch, to heal, to hatch, to heal.

Dark Room

1.

His camera lens, stippled with mist
from the flume, exposed the wind's motions
and a distant out-of-focus deer
that grazed the film, while nearby
she stretched out in the shade.

2.

For years they coexisted in his case
(symbiotic within silver slivers)
as if forsaking faith in days
to wait in the negative.

3.

There was loss: their image of family
darkened by arguments over Christ.
The projector flashing early trips
couldn't flip history fast enough
to overtake the pace of change.

Someone always walked across the light.

4.

Once, he kept his shutter open too long
and light gushed through. The morning star
scoring the night film disappeared
into white sky. He wanted it to be
God, but it was gone.

FAMILY PHOTO, CIRCA 1975

We kids with our mother in wind: her hair adrift,
flagging out like tethered, uncertain talk from her
red bandanna, on Mt. Monadnock. All of us
followed faded white paint on granite stones that marked
the ascent. Our father's off-frame
shadow falling from his perspective, taking us
in, his lens adjusted to frame the background. Clouds
browse the summit, us three kids, and her, looking sore,
staring down but smiling faintly, as though she knew
someday we would see and remember her back then,
still with us and granite, a man that sharp and hard.

The Oath

A winter's anger found us among pines
along the trail beside Spit Brook,

where fractures in the knife-thin ice exposed
a flowing darkness we saw in water

that day we swore the oath. Then we took off.
Beyond our back yard, the hill breached

low clouds infiltrating thick scrub
that gave way to weeds and a run-down shack.

When the woman who trapped rabbits there
chased us three runaways off her land,

we ran home, we children of the hill,
past rabbits hung along the path.

We zigzagged to avoid her snares,
our weaving tangled up with sounds

of jeans brushing past the undergrowth
and corduroys sawing into the distance.

Breathless and steaming in the cold, we felt
our blood flow from the stinging knife-cuts

along our palms, where we had sealed the oath
that we would never be like grown-ups were.

In Silence

Our steps developed voids
when autumn air got trapped
in cavities that day
concrete was poured into
the form our father had made
while he smoked a cigarette.
From too much water
or sand in the mix, a void
became a hole through the years,
a familiar gap concrete framed.
It had expanded
as blue smoke rings did
beyond his mouth: in silence
slowly echoed. One summer,
snakes siphoned out of
the gloomy space inside the steps,
through what he called a hell
of a hole, as though
his grim inner critic
flicked its tongue from him
to us. "What a joke,"
he said, "What a joke,"
then turned, tight-lipped,
and walked into the woods.

The Woods

We would split there.
Our parents
never could find
our footprints
in the ways we went—
through words,
in trouble—
to wrestle wood,
to drag long fallen branches
homeward
with our calloused hands.
We wrote with our blood
on birch.

HIDE AND SEEK

To disappear was just a choice
to self-select or self-destruct
in woods where everyone was "it."

Most often, I would try to hide
my body from some ancient threat—
a wrathful word or demon thought—

but never did succeed. That is,
I tried, I tried incredibly
to stop my breath under the steps,

in burnt-out trees, in shrubbery,
behind a dark, imagined fabric
on a million-mile laundry line

under staring stars or the spurs
of galaxies, but when alone,
at last, I always found myself.

WAKE: 1978

Maybe it's an urban myth
that the ice cream man comes with
drugs up his sleeve, crack and speed
in packets with lick sticks, beads
of ecstasy on necklace strings,
yet she hears the truck coming
from three blocks away, tosses
her books into the long stalks
of timothy and yellow
poppies along the path, throws
her head back, then sprints home
to beg for another loan
until allowance day.
She enters the house crazed,
shouting. They all understand.
Everyone sits holding hands
beside the uncovered
box in which her brother
from this day on will lie.
She looks toward his eyes
at the coins placed in the way
of his chronically blood-shot gaze,
which eyedrops couldn't wash off,
then reaches for the coins in awe—

Platonic Seesaw

We never touched our middles, or touched them
from extremes, but sat off-kilter,
   or so I seemed. You straddled near the end
and kicked your pumps for oil. I slid in some
   to find the Golden Mean. (You were the girl
for me.) I slid too far at first—I was
   heavier that year—and perched, astonished
at a glimpse of your brassiere. I pushed up, felt light
   as you kicked and bucked my body down.
I tried again to balance us—that fulcrum was
   too fair. I inched into a splinter
that needled up my leg. You dizzied me
   as my hamstring bled. Your lips broke then
into a sparing smile. And then you moved ten miles away.
   Between our centers summer never moved,
or moved in painful wisdom kids possess,
   occult and mean. I forget your name.

A Wake

When it began, the blue jays called out from the trees,
then chainsaws cut through bark, spitting dust from their teeth.
Anonymous half-visible men stood in clouds
and cleared the woods to build houses behind our house,
decades concealed. Surveyors vaguely gleaned from two
decayed markers that a graveyard, which none of us knew
existed, had been hidden in those woods. Some ghosts
exited when the excavators got too close.
Their faces grimaced within shadows on my wall.
Those heirs of anxiety crept around, appalled
by error-ridden plans for basements soon to cross
barriers that had long confined their bones, now lost.
By evening, twitches and tics floated through my vision.
Believing briefly in those hallucinations
led me to sense the slender branches of a birch
dreadfully reach into the room and merge
with my nerve endings. Then I waited for saws to cut
the pith at dawn, as unprepared for what
morning brought as for night: the unobstructed sky,
more light when other trees swayed and cracked nearby.
To turn again into the breezy boy I was
tutored not to be that night, I drifted up, then saw
a charm of finches swell off the roof, seemingly

alarmed, as if they flew from my final dreaming.
At once they veered from where the canopy had stretched,
as one, contracting back again, down to a hedge.
Bewildered by the space where days before I could
see wilderness, I faced a memory of woods,
a honeysuckle scent, but saw logs hauled away
by trucks. And suddenly I knew I was awake.

Blood Cemetery

How brief and inarticulate the speech
of those stones which like jawless teeth
irrupt the lawns of our cemeteries.

—William Gass
"The Soul Inside the Sentence"

Abel Blood, 1797-1867

We went in search of Blood among the old
headstones—a name passed down from the beyond,
before times, orally—hooked by the lore
of an unverified ghost, after life,
while our lives hovered still, a dreadful list
of acts that would soon thrust us unsurely
toward other, unknown states. It was a test
to see if we could be susceptible
to an immortal soul, which local tales
took on faith. So, we put our senses up
to it, in the essence of that darkness,
our faces close to stones surrounded once
by wilderness, a row of them like worn,
ground teeth, and between them we living met

a self-revealing end in the blood flooding
through our arteries, then vitally
departed through the few remaining trees.

ADOLESCENCE

That night the inescapable
humidity transformed us as
we trespassed past the barbed wire fence
and felt our fear suffused with blood.

We grazed our skin on the tall grass
that closed behind us, then we saw
mosquitoes take our sacrifice
and fill themselves with drops of us,

initiates to what we did
not know. We broke past cattails, punks,
and found the ruined friary
whose windows let us see inside

a darkness, incomplete because
the moonlight made it through, although
our vision could not help us know
the heedless, hidden reason we

had disappeared into that field,
had scared the scarce wilderness off

into the skeletal woods that
looked etched in sky by a witch.

More than once we mistook glimmers
for something moving through the marsh
beyond our dark-adapted sight,
by then the light the thing to fear.

In a Ward

In a dream I climbed through the pine tree canopy
into clouds that looked like silence materialized.

There I was trying to repair a fault of time
expressed by broken light. I scaled with ladders

propped on an illuminated branch of brain cells
or photons that later misted into darkness,

flickered out when they touched the underlying night.
With blankets whose rung-like folds I had climbed kicked off,

and stars all covered by my grasp of where I woke,
I plunged from dream, or what of it I could remember, cold.

THE CARPENTER

I remember when I fell from that rafter
sunlight hung on an angle through the window
and a strip of lead broke the light
into two sheets divided by a rod of shade.
In my falling I tried to grab the shade, as if
that thin ghost of a frame would save me

simply because my hand could fit around it.
The wide and hardly graspable light
blinded me as I dropped to the pinewood floor.
Later, the same light woke me and was a comfort
while the shade only chilled me
with a memory of my body.

Jane Kenyon in March

1. Synapses

—March 3, 1988

Good thing my grandmother asked,
after my mind turned to wood,
"Would you write to him?" because
saws, I believed, cut through it,
literally, termites gnawed
my thoughts. Her letters would ease
at least my need for other
theories about things that eat
at reason. Thus our friendship
depended mainly on words
in cursive—small, like nerve ends.
Then that was the way. Within
hints of her lifelong anguish
she conveyed an unflinching
affinity on that date,
created paths on paper
predisposed to the innate
relation of thought and flesh.
Let me hear from you, she said.

2. UNDER THUNDER CLOUDS

I've just heard thunder for the first time
in six months....It has turned terribly dark.
                              —March 18, 1989

Precursors to what the clouds
could have signaled was a curse
first came like April's forecast.
Weeks passed with *no daffodils...*
cold wind every day. She crashed.
Ash-colored signals flew south.
Now I'm in that nowhere place...
in...bad shape—for months. Somehow
out of it she wrote me with
pithy comments and questions,
gestures that served as rhythmic
lithium to me. *I feel*
as if a UFO landed
in the back yard. Mercifully
uplifted from summer's rut,
suffused with joy by Advent—
she had taught me to adjust.
Rusty UFOs hovered,
however, below the clouds.

3. FLATTENED

—*March 19, 1990*

Twice that day in her cryptic
script she wrote with a concise,
slantwise urgency, *Call me...*
Although an anxious appeal,
a plea, her melancholy
calmness held the lines on both
postcards, sent two days after
her pastor's death. They were close,
mostly friends, and she had rushed
(she later wrote) right at his
illness, but then he *vanished*,
ushered at dusk through the fuse
of suffering to the *bright
lights of annihilation.*
Secluded in her attic
office that Monday morning,
mourning in her words, she sat,
flattened, beginning to call
to local and far-flung friends.

4. Episodes

—March 25, 1991

During winter and the first
Persian Gulf War, she endured,
under covers, side effects
and specters of the abyss.
Physically I am a wreck.
Iraq was too. (She opposed
the supposed national
rationale of that episode,
in prose.) After the cease-fire,
her spirits better, she still
felt ill—more deeply mired in
regimens of chemicals
inimical to her peace,
her mind's equanimity—
animated but dismayed,
saying *I could go to bed
and never get up*...Waylaid
some days, she was having it
out with melancholy then.

5. More Tests

They can't tell me what it is.
          —*March 24, 1992*

Scarcely a word of sorrow,
that sparrow dying mid-air.
If spared that, now she fell *sick*
in cycles—a consequence,
she sensed, of psychotropics
mixed with the start of normal
hormonal changes—and yet
tests showed no anomalies.
Dormant bees would soon emerge
to forage maple blossoms
hummingbirds probed surgically,
but purgatorial crud
that mud season made her wait
to rake, for peony buds,
for her blood work to come back,
active one week, running Gus
uphill, the next out of whack.
Blackspot lay in wait in spores.
Unsure, she would *get sick, lie low…*

6. WORRY WORDS

Tell him the page I didn't write…
—Dickinson, "The Letter"

—February 18, 1993

—April 14, 1993

A gap. A few states apart—
inarticulate synapse,
an absence foretold, and not
forgotten, since not written
or sent. My year hectic, fraught.
Blots of ink. My mind annealed
and healing, slowly. The brief
fibers of her letters reeled
ideally off a spindle
the wind turned. An interview,
a TV crew. Soon again
to India. A new book.
But hooked to the ends, disjunct
punctuation I mistook
for continuity…while
my files filled with her worry
for me in endless exile,
miles and miles from home. *Dear,
are you <u>there</u>?? We are <u>here</u>!*

7. TERMINAL SCRIPT

—March 8, 1994
(Nearly the same day she wrote
her note six years earlier.)

Dear, I have leukemia…

Immediately her voice
poised in air came back to me,
meeting my memory—her
letter, two years before this,
whispering *bone pain* and her,
heroic on the couch, once
confessing "My bones hurt." Signs
in spring from her mind's frontier.
One year after…it was March,
our last meeting in the flesh,
yes?—but this the last postmarked,
archived touch of pale blue ink.

—Inclining my head, I read
each indistinct letter. Words
sink. *Love*—almost a flat line,
final, yet still legible.

P.S.

Proctor Cemetery, Andover, NH

On roads I traveled sometimes,
smitten like you, through the snow,
over frost heaves, I come to

your tombstone where now I must
summon you from depth into
intuition. The old fence

presents an iron figure
girding you, like a defense,
a difference between life

stifled and one discovered
over decades of loose strife
and knife-edge analysis.

Persistently there, my friend,
not alien, you guide this
one mystifying breath toward

words, again. For years, too long,
I wrongly thought my inward
war for balance would sunder

this undertaking, and us.

INFLUENCE

Driving to Walden Pond
we took back roads we never would have known
had solipsism been our way.
Some bad directions led us off
the thoroughfare too soon
and after straying for a mile we found

a modern sculpture park, where figures lay
like armored corpses in the woods
near exhibition halls
and a tower skeined with vines.
In a field, among the sculptures, we laughed
self-consciously about the head

of "Rising Cairn" (a metal cage
shaped like a life-sized man
filled with stones), whose stones we could remove
and replace, as if they were memories.
And we forgot our lack of time
while thinking we were close

to history, until
yellow jackets scared us into the car,

eventually. With a sense
that self-preservation depends
on shifting interests,
through more wrong turns we made it to the plots

of Concord's authors: Thoreau's and others.
The buzz at Sleepy Hollow was
from mowers. Marvelous
lines of the famous dead
with rusted chains for barriers around
their headstones, and the unknown rest

traversed the cemetery's hills.
We scanned their epitaphs
and names for hours, sniffling now and then, due
to hay fever, mainly. Their influence
naturally caused our consciousness
to itch...

Shade collected like silt
from light filtered by the mountain laurels,
and it fell to us to neglect
the apprehension of it all,
since we felt a need to
experience the pond. Why we had gone

to see the misplaced empty replica
of a self-built house walled-in by pines
was, inadvertently,
to serve its preservation,
but then to disobey anxieties
derived from simple deference

to water's fatal qualities—
that is, to swim. We skimmed
the words Thoreau had used to criticize
society, then headed to the woods
to find the original site
in a cove. We saw

the water sway to us
and waded in. Still it was not too late.
We threw out some stones, ones
he might have known, the leavings of
an ancient glacier,
then made our way back.

LIVING UNDERGROUND

Two years in the basement within
earshot of the oil furnace, always
hot and on my own, I cooked in
the coal bin converted by my quiet
old Jewish landlords into a kitchen.
Through the doorway I heard a jet
and gawked at a bomb-struck convoy—
hawk-eye of the news camera
high above Kuwait to avoid
the flak—then saw my only visitor
scrappily emerge from a void
below the fireplace, where I stored
the TV: a grayish house mouse
peeked up like an unorthodox
superhero, looking nervous.
I froze. Just when on the screen there
rose pillars of smoke from anonymous
still figures in the desert theater,
the daring mouse darted under
blaring planes in Kuwait's airspace.
Kingdoms depended on its run.
It slipped into a narrow gap
gypsum boards made, as a manhunt

with Humvees started, and perhaps
it snuck up the chimney or out a vent.
Hushed and brooding, I ate supper,
managed to draft a polemic, then
in turmoil tried to sleep. In the dark,
murmurs from upstairs and the efficient
furnace mixed. Outside a dog barked.

After an Attack

I thought I'd go out to listen
to what people were saying,
not to get involved or betray
myself, but to hear what I'd missed
of rumors in our town
after so long. I thought
I'd go out. I thought I ought
to go out but not make a sound,
in order to preserve a calm
and a state from which to hear
the tone of the voices there
without losing my sense of song
or whatever stood for it
those days. I thought I'd try to sense
from my neighbors the difference
events had made. I thought I'd sit
on a bench outside and bother
to hear at least the noise that planes,
and ferries, and trucks on the two-lane
highway made, as other
subtler sounds and bodies passed
for a pattern by the buildings
still there. I thought I'd note things

such as swaying coral maples, hats,
the pleasant slope of some streets
toward the lake, a house with sunrise
splayed across its clapboards, surprise
the many pears caused on their tree,
the cast of shadows created
from wooden signs in the park,
the broken lattice arch
dangling near the dilapidated
greenhouse blotched with a dark moss,
the effect of that, and the way
the current of those days
had sounded, looked, and felt like loss.
I thought, I thought, and I thought.

The Protocol

Convincing people not to kill themselves
will teach you how to breathe: slowly, deeply,
in deference to the act. They know
exactly why they have guitar string strung
around their necks, and you can never understand
their loss by following the protocols
you know. Typically, they tell you only
in wispy clues: "My mother died", or "I
really want to fall asleep." A suspect wish
should be your cue to ask if they're thinking
of killing themselves, as matter-of-factly
as you'd ask if they're going on vacation
this year. Do not reveal your fear. Long silence
equals "Yes." Take a deep breath, then assess
the risk: "Did you plan this for tonight?
Before? With a shotgun? Do you have one?"
Ask them to keep their pills out of reach.
Suggest that they take a deep breath. Be sure
you have plenty of time before you ask:
"Have you tried this in the past?" Sometimes
they talk until they're bored with thoughts
of death. You listen for their weaknesses
and breathe with them between their words, alone

but loud enough for them to hear. Never
say, "I care." Never talk about yourself.
And never put a suicide on hold.
There comes a time to broach eternity:
"It can wait a day, don't you agree?"
Ask about nights they've survived the dark when
no options floated into view. "You can
always kill yourself tomorrow, but how
can you unwind the string right now?"
Distraction's not the least of tactics you can use
to persuade them not to act: "Go see
the arboretum cherry trees in bloom.
Play some pool." If the threat is imminent—
a loaded gun, a foot outside a window, a breeze
whistling through the receiver—the breathing trick
won't do; they've got all the air
they need. You calmly ask: "What do you see?
Any signs? Buildings? Which bank is that?"
Determine where they live by any means
you can. The protocol develops wings.
No other call demands such cunning: "You won't
believe this, but someone's at our door..."
Then call the police on another phone.
Maybe you'll hear the ironic sirens,
the knock, the door coming down, their rage
betrayed again. For those devoted few,
the savvy who won't give you any clues,

who threaten to hang up—leap
into a guilt trip: "What about your kids?
How will they live with the hole you blow
into their lives? What will God think? Please tell me
I haven't wasted my time." Only when you've tried
all other swaying acts and charming breaths
do you put the bullet guilt in their hands
to toss aside again, until they give
the protocol, and you, another chance to breathe.
And even then you never know how long
they live after the call, what hell they gauge
each day. You have to accept that.

A Living

Out it's cast—
the fish lure's eye
stares back
and forth,
depending on
my wrist,
the angle it
describes
on the static
present
rippling past.
The river
there is time,
there is time,
and I,
recurring
in its water,
can't escape
the lure's look,
its hook,
the nylon
waves in air,
a sine,

a cloud's
outline,
a tightrope
sound
whispers
on, into
the beyond.

CARP

At dawn, dashes of rain
began to nick Spit Brook.
A carp rose toward air,
breached. (Where the surface broke

a mouth of water yawned.)
Then it slipped down until
fully swallowed and gone,
much like a morning pill.

Surfacing

That heat. By dusk we leapt
into the sea, to disappear beneath
the horizon: our held

breath something like belief.
All around us depth and pressure. Without
boundary, no meaning

floated: nothing to grip.
Thinking: *no help. Breathe. Stay up* and *forget
thinking*—no time for that

crest well above my head
going under: until my backup brain
came back up. What luck. Then

the pivot: like a fin
remembered in my hand, back when. Visions
of liquid, then land. Light:

lost inside the trough. *Not
yet...not*—yet, with a surge: a stroke, a breath.
Others somewhere in sound.

Rhythm from a distance
eons gone. Swells that rocked my body, soon
bloodied, up onto rocks

where darkness rested, where
motions from all directions collided
to offset themselves. *Still*

here—thrown to rocks I held
till others reappeared and noisily
we breathed. Some air: some sea.

THEY COME

—the maidenhair ferns

Out back, the ferns have cloned themselves
and hordes have inched in to surround
my patio with blades that graze
the window's glass.
                    Impersonal,
the plants defy the metaphor
that banished them to human terms
as maidens (buried upright to their heads
apparently),
                    but all because
medieval fern-like people bound
them to us with a term, a stalk
long-dead brains bore, I sense them creep
like zombies through the years, through soil.

Their ragged shocks of hair tremble
in wind…and now they block the path.

QUAKING ASPEN

A massive body shifted earth
    along a fault, but what we saw
        were sawtooth aspen leaves, a swarm
as from a wasp-nest, and their wrath
    was wrong, was what we felt: the force
        that made the heart-shaped leaves tremble
first made our too-trained minds rebel
    then petrified us. It got worse:
        Wave trains warped the street, cracked asphalt,
split brick, and through a gaping, gasping
    collective cardiac arrest,
        the last train took our breath and left.

        Rush hour, upended, ended up
    our rush to get across the street
to our assembly point: the tree.
        We gauged each other, our workgroup,
    to spot when the uprooted stems
of our buried nervous systems
        would wiggle back down into our
    own faults and cavities on routes
the shocks shook through, as if we were
        the earthquake's shape, which the aspen

had seemed when energy ascended
its pith after the ground fractured.

Meanwhile, our joggled chests and skulls
    vibrated still, our bodies vehicles
        of a sense of the size of things
beyond our bones and skin reflecting
    the aspen's branches and the leaves
        it demonstrated wavelengths with.
These facts upset the widespread myth
    of individuality
        and separateness. Experience
the tremors triggered brought us
    suddenly to a common sense:
        It was not The Big One. No, not yet.

Swoop

The vibration around my head felt as if it came from thinking, or a muscle in my skull relaxing, then I heard a sound: momentum: wings, in a second, caught up in the word *swoop*: so close to my head that when they appeared in front of me I thought my eyebrows had flown off: though what went from my head the way a word would instantly wasn't me or mine, or intimate, but bird, crow, flying off tangent, banking toward a sycamore: simply seeming to have made a playful choice, almost to have asked me to trust it, as a knife-thrower might have: to have asked me to wake up: though it hadn't even done that: and yet I felt it to be an extension of here, here an extension of now, now an extension of my attention then: but almost mystically independent, as mystical as anything is independent.

Air Graffiti

Walking, I saw sneakers tap dance on power lines
and asphalt cracks in the shape of Nepal;
a skirt, a long burgundy skirt
of amaranth and memories entwined
                    on Thomas Street; and how the small
                swallows looped and flew in cursive-like
            billows of air graffiti that spelled grace.
I thought to breathe, and breathed, flushing out grief

that surfaced, unexpected and intense:
            the feeling we humans are a disgrace
                to nature. Moments later, in a breeze
                    a plum fell from a tree near the garden.
Aplomb, I thought (small bomb set off inside
my head), *is not enough for us to bear
this fall*. I turned to see what else the birds
might write: blue-green streaks in the evening air.

Aversive Therapy

A condor claws at men when they are men,
but when they wear their man-made condor heads
it watches cautiously.
                            The men make life
repulsive, dangerous, as men, as here
a condor learns again how not to trust,
oblivious to trickery as long
as men stay men when men and never show
their transformation.
                            In the dark of night
a calf appears—fresh kill—but then a hand
where hands should not have been attracts its eye
and moves: an error that corrupts. Its claws
contract.
                The men try not to be
themselves, they must become themselves again
and instigate its fear.
                            It must not know
who feeds it, nor the care they took to fool
its instinct back from where it was distracted
in the first place, by men and what they did.

May Snow

Secretly we all felt let down by nature
when the snowfall failed to accumulate.
We wanted something deep to touch, to have
to acclimate to, and to help us exercise
the old survival skills our jobs cover up
in cities. With so many moving flakes
to project our wonder onto, we felt
employed by and large with an easy care
warm people who own multitudes of things
can entertain. "It's beautiful!" High up,
we watched its pace increase, as if it were
the ghost of instinct struggling to emerge.

Yet more fantastically, the millions
of flakes appeared to perforate the wet
blacktop's event horizon for a second
then disappear. As if we lingered on
a boundless planet not cartwheeling
through a void, we casually stood by
the window as they fell: just crystallized
ice and dust specks that caused the cool feeling
that they continued, intact, into

a vast unconscious inner space,
a mental galaxy they penetrated,
but left us hazardless, at risk from nothing.

MOGULS

As skiers know, it's best to fall in action—
  that way you have momentum
to keep your spine a fulcrum
  during the unavoidable contraction
of all your muscles into
  the moguls, which will slow you
in the jarring manner of unyielding facts

that mark the overthrow of falling bodies
  but flip you various ways
such that if you're good, and wise,
  you'll find a way to twist into the odd
condition of recovery—
  pole tips back, your knees bent over
your toes—and think you brushed against a god

to do it; otherwise, you just fall down
  while standing there, with wasted speed,
without your edges in or a need
  for the dynamics that you could have found
to give you certain mystical
  perspectives and the crucial skill
to see past yourself as you rose from the ground.

Avalanche Season

Back when I gravitated
toward the deep to counter my lofty thoughts,
    I skied as ash
    leaned in a bowl with the wet weight
of thawing snow. My dog-mind wandered off.
    It always has
    moments of forecast-like absence
that hazily imply the risk of doom
    that only it
    could grasp, if it were present.
Little ellipses of snow rolled down ungroomed
    faces, and yet
    still I held a sinuous line
instantly broken when my inside edge
    caught and I fell
    head first. Here I would be lying
if I said I could share a wise adage.
    I scared myself.
    All I had were elbows and poles
and attitude. Instinctively I dug
    an elbow in,
    then wrenched upright, pointed downslope
on the fall line, and could not have been judged

at ease again,
because I saw a sheet of snow
collapse beside my line, below. It sloughed
much the way
a slacker metaphor could now:
the adolescent sees he must strip off
the many layers
of defense in which he tucked mistakes.
Except, it slid down threateningly real.
When finally
I reached the crater's snow-topped lake
and rose from my tuck, I began to feel
for injuries,
looked upwards, had a mind to watch
for further slides, thought better of that plan,
then quit those woods.

Moth in a Red Bell Pepper

Ventriloquist, be still! I hear your flapping,
dull tongue of the inner world.
My ventricles flutter just like you
inside my heart. Cut it out. *Cut it out.*

FLY

Look at *Fly*: the trivial arms of *y*
thrown up at the end to help us see
the avenues of escape, its stem
submerged like a rudder caught in ice,

or flapping there after a failure
of feathers, haughty, compensating,
dragging its lesser letters onward
by concentrating, like a root in fall

from which a *v* still ramifies,
but stalls, stuck up in a false victory,
begging, "Why me?" or merely, "Why?"

Behind the wall of *l*, which dams the *y*'s
retreat, *F* stands to fight with gravity
and criticize its flunked attempt at sky.

MARTIAL ARTIST

I inherited a knack for catching falling things:
a light bulb my friend dropped from her ceiling,
someone's scarf in windy weather…

It's a martial art of courtesy, and I'm its martyr.
Why did my ancestors bring this skill into the world?
Which of them had to save their plunging child?

GOSSIP

At the library I opened
Chronicle of a Death Foretold
and found a moth jammed inside,
caught in the spine, but alive,
squirming in Spanish,
its wings imprinted
with the mirror of memory,
and when I flicked it from the trap
I imagined it flew off to gossip
with generations of moths
about the weight of words
and suffocating pleasures
of pages of beautiful phrases
about desperation and betrayal
which it overheard whispered
through the paper
between words speaking
to each other, wondering why
this interloping moth
had anything to do
with Santiago Nasar on page 22
when it was already evident
he was doomed.

BURIAL MOUND

Once inside the tomb
I called to my echo
to second the sound
only those walls
produced, a bass
hidden in my voice
behind anxiety,

and when I called
the swallows came,
singing me back
as from the dead,
from the darkness
I did not want to leave
beyond the arch,

which they would not
pass under, and so
they flew, high-pitched,
outside that drum
I hummed in, calling
to me in the tones
of far-off traumas.

THE END OF MOURNING

This morning, I spotted my dead sister
in a crowded café in a French village.
There she was, breezing out the door,
and I leapt from my seat to follow her
into the cobbled street, shouting "Mary!"
When she turned, she stared at me
with vague recognition, as one might
after not seeing her younger brother
for ten years, after assuming
another personality, elsewhere.
Impersonally, she beamed, "I'm dead!" Then,
thrilled as she could be at a fantastic thought,
"I love it!" Seeing she was about to run off,
disinterested in the living,
I woke, noting that, apparently,
she is having the time of her afterlife.

A LETTER TO ALIENS

•— • —• • • —•• —•— ——— ••— •—•

•••• • •—•• •——•

The little bit of hope up my sleeve fell
and there it lay: a glossy red spaceship,
apparently a fake, a diamond shape
on a trick card that made me whisper, "Well,
we might as well stay in this, don't you think?"
My partner at the table had fallen asleep.
While counting cards or mutilated sheep
she slipped into oblivion. I took a drink,
false landing gear of light came heaven-sent
from a green lamp, and there in my best hand
two figures gleamed: a heart and the diamond.
Sadly I played the heart, but no one went
for it. Now would you please come out of the blue
we see around this modest chunk of dust,
where with a little bit of hope and not much trust
we've tried to win the future? We are due.
And not in aerofoils made of tin,
but come in social swallows, come in oaks.
"Come in, come in," we'll say, "Come meet the folks."
You'll discourse for a moment on our sins

by dropping leaves or flying in an arc
that nearly sickles through our necks. We'll stake
our lives on yours. To help us pray, you'll make
a nest inside our heads. You'll forgive on a lark.

POET ANONYMOUS

For the same reason I will not run
for President
I no longer rhyme: I can't afford to.

They are expensive, those words that ring
my tocsin heart.
They cost me jobs selling watches and cars

plus commodity talk used to swing
deals in dark bars
in D.C. Put me up at the P.A.

and they accrue so much interest
the sounds don't stop
until hawks pierce them with squawking nonsense

no sane caucus would ever elect.
So I'm caught here
in the eternal smear campaign of sound—

less my partner in crime (my vice echo)
to ride shotgun
as the hawks refuse the crumbs I throw.

LAMBORGHINI POEM

I refuse to look at Lamborghinis,
because Lamborghinis are driven
to be seen. In a Lamborghini is
a man with a Lamborghini need
demanding "Look at me!" despite the tint
on his hip-high windows. I know people
who look down to see a Lamborghini
regardless of the time of day. They whip
around or stop to wonder whose it is,
as if Picasso had wrecked a sunset
and mounted it on wheels for their betterment.
I don't blame them. They are my friends. Their bus
could be delayed, and a Lamborghini
may be better than the usual sun
set down across the sound, if they know their bus is
late, or just will never come this damned time.
Still, I refuse. One superficial dent
can send a fancy car to the shop.
I rev that thought. As a Lamborghini
I refuse to look at creeps in the park,
a sufficient sun wanders by us and is
the wonder I choose as I wait for my bus.

The Dancer

Huddled inside our brief cases
of awe and award-worthy self-
control, we watched him in the aisle
dance with a boxer's sense of style
to the infusion of music
that bled from his headphones to us.
He mixed in fist pumps with rhythmic jabs
at shadows and a taxicab
whose passenger looked up, appalled.
With one hand he flashed the sign
for "Stop," faked like he was scratching
a wavy groove along the glass
as we crossed Broadway, then reached up
and plucked the cord, in time, the bell
to end the round. When the bus stopped
he composed himself and jumped off
into the night to disappear,
appearing to be struck by the lights.

MAJOR PHILOSOPHY

After the graduation party
she flashed for several blocks in sequins,
reflecting on everybody,

until an officer cut in and said
through his cruiser's bullhorn: "I can't believe
you're gonna jaywalk *right
in front of me.* Didn't you see my lights?!"

She could have been forgiven
for not seeing them apart from ones
that looked emitted from within her,

but she put forth a masterful defense with her
enlightened smile when he repeated
"I can't believe…," then with arms akimbo
she replied in sequence "I know, I know…"

ARRIVAL

At last I can see through myself:
twilit in the train, transparent

in the glass, my reflection lets
me see the world outside through what

I wear: I swear the ground below
moves left while we inside move right

into the darkness letting go
gradually: gradually

the dimmest light appears within
my chest: and as we pull into

the station, people there peer through
my face, in shadows, which I face.

GETTING YOU OFF

I was dusting the blinds blind
because the sun was in my eyes
that day I had or took off.

Blindly I was dusting the blinds,
getting myself off and wishing
it was your dust too, but you had
never been there to shed.

My mind was elsewhere, with you,
and all the particles of our life
together, until life did us part,

were flying. I was dusting over
them and under them. I was under-
going it and being over it.

I was under-being and going
over it again and again, in strokes
both quick and slow, by feel.

When my mind returned, I took it
I was blindly dusting the blinds
because of a reflection.
It hit the window through the wind.

Slowly I was dusting
the blinds, and when I was done
I shut them, twisted the rod
and quickly opened my eyes

to see how much I had, how much
I had gotten off. I could barely hear
the sweeping wind taking you with it
elsewhere then, when I was done.

AFTER THOUGHT

heal: OE hál. hale, whole

Along a crack   a white clay bowl
in the deep sink   split in my hands:
the breath-like sound   of a skullcap
a coroner   cut and pried off.
Through the window   my thoughts flew up
on a thermal   into the night,
beyond one pane   partially cranked
open—outward,   at an angle—
as abrasive   overtones of
a landing plane   passed overhead.
Mirrored in glass,   my sideways face
drew my eyes left,   directly toward
its dead ringer,   dimples and all:
me too, but square   in front of me
in the hingeless   half of window,
hovering there.   How long it took
that frame of mind   to form, to fill.
I reached my fingers   forward to
the crank, wound it   clockwise, a kind
of surgery to   sew together
those selves exposed   as separate but

created or   cast from my one
vantage point—there   where in theory
I thrived, although   thought had the means
to perplex me,   to portray me
otherwise. Only   afterthought
acted as an airway,   opened on
that process, as the plane's noise died.

ACKNOWLEDGMENTS

Many thanks to the editors of the publications in which the following poems first appeared, sometimes in different versions:

American Literary Review: "Fly"
The American Scholar: "Lamborghini Poem"
Blue Press: "After an Attack" and "They Come"
Case Reserve Review: "The Oath"
Consequence: "Living Underground"
English Journal: "Gossip"
Harvard Review: "A Letter to Aliens"
The Maine Review: "Adolescence"
New Letters: "The Carpenter"
Ninth Letter: "Swoop"
Notre Dame Review: "Influence" and "Jane Kenyon in March"
Ploughshares: "Dark Room" and "Yesterday I Wrote a Poem Called 'Yesterday'"

Poet Lore: "The Protocol" and "Wake: 1978"

Poetry Northwest: "Poet Anonymous"

Prism Review: "Hide and Seek" and "In a Ward"

Salt Hill: "Moth in a Red Bell Pepper"

Self-Portrait: Poetry on Buses: "Martial Artist"

Smartish Pace: "Getting You Off"

Sport Literate: "Moguls"

The Texas Review: "Platonic See Saw"

Weber—The Contemporary West: "Aversive Therapy"

Welter: "The Dancer"

Thanks, also, to Bruce Beasley, Heather McHugh, Radha Marcum, Derek Sheffield, and Jeanne Yeasting for their invaluable comments on early drafts of some of these poems, to Danielle Jones of Yas Press for generous advice on them, to Jennifer Militello for selecting this book for the Granite State Poetry Prize, and to Molly McGrath and Ashley Halsey of Pink Eraser Press for their splendid editorial production and design of it. A special thanks to the YAS Foundation for supporting the publication of this book.

THE NOSSRAT YASSINI POETRY FESTIVAL at UNH celebrates the power of poetry to unify, bring people together, and build a better community. Poetry is the oldest literary art form and the one we turn to in times of great joy, sorrow, and inspiration. Because we treasure and remember the poems that have influenced our lives, celebrating poetry can bring us together in uniquely powerful ways. This world class festival brings together poets, students, teachers, and poetry lovers of all kinds to experience the poetic richness of New Hampshire and the New England community.

Yᴀꜱ Pʀᴇꜱꜱ, housed in the University of New Hampshire's English department, publishes three books a year featuring the best poetry in New Hampshire: an anthology of teen poetry, an anthology of USNH student poetry, and a previously unpublished poetry collection of extraordinary quality written by an emerging or established New Hampshire poet. These prize-winning publications are made possible through the generous support of the YAS Foundation in honor of poet and poetry lover, Nossrat Yassini. In addition, The Nossrat Yassini Poetry Prize—an annual award given each year to a first book published by a U.S. poet of extraordinary promise—is managed by the Press.

yas press

THOM SCHRAMM grew up in New Hampshire. His poems have appeared in many magazines, including *AGNI*, *The American Scholar*, *Harvard Review*, and *Ploughshares*, and have won an Academy of American Poets Prize. He is the editor of *Living in Storms: Contemporary Poetry and the Moods of Manic-Depression* (Eastern Washington University Press, 2008) and author of *The Leaf Blower* (Blue Cubicle Press, 2016).